Java
Learn The Basics In

3 Days

DAVID CHANG

ISBN-10: 1548937843
ISBN-13: 978-1548937843

CONTENTS

FUNDAMENTALS OF OBJECT ORIENTED PROGRAMMING

1.1 INTRODUCTION (OOP)

Object Oriented Programming (OOP) is an approach to standardize the programs by creating partitioned memory area for both data and method. It has been developed to increase the programmer's productivity and also to overcome the traditional approach of programming. The different Object Oriented Programming languages are C++, Java, Simula-67, etc.

An Object Oriented Programming (OOP) allows the data to be applied within designated program area. It gives more significance to data rather than Methods which means it also provides the reusability feature to develop productive logic.

FEATURES OF OBJECT ORIENTED PROGRAMMING (OOP)

- The objects can be used as a bridge to have data flow from one method to another.
- It gives importance to data items rather than methods.
- It makes the complete program simpler by dividing it into a number of objects.
- Data can be easily modified without any change in the method.

PRINCIPLES OF (OOP)

- Objects
- Classes
- Data Abstraction
- Encapsulation
- Data Hiding
- Inheritance
- Polymorphism

1.2 OBJECTS AND CLASSES

OBJECTS

Object is a unique entity which contains data and methods (characteristics and behavior) together in an Object Oriented Programming (OOP) Language.

Example: Let us consider the real world objects, which are visible before us.

Any object in the real world can possess the following characteristics:

- It is visible.
- It can be described easily.

You can observe that the above mentioned criteria has unique identity,   definite state, or characteristics and behaviors. For example consider an object Bed:

It has the following characteristics:

- It has four legs.
- It has a plain top.

And the behaviors are:

- It is used to sleep.
- It is used to sit.

In Payroll system, an employee may be taken as an example of object where **characteristics** are name, designation, basic pay and **behavior** as calculating gross pay, provident fund, printing pay slip, etc.

CLASSES

Class is a set of different objects. Class can contain fields and methods to explain about the behavior of an object. Each object of a class possesses same attributes and behavior defined within the same class. Class is also termed as Object factory.

For Example: If Rainbow is the class then the colors in the rainbow represent the different objects of the class Rainbow.

Similarly, we can consider a class named fruit where apple, mango, orange are members of the class fruit. If fruit is defined as a class, then the statement:

fruit apple = new fruit(); will create an object apple belonging to the class fruit.

1.3 DATA ABSTRACTION

Abstraction refers to the act of representing essential features (relevant data) without including background details in order to reduce complexity and increase efficiency.

Abstraction is the absolute property of a class. The class binds the data items and functions to promote abstraction. The data members are accessed only through the related methods. A class uses the property of abstraction called as **abstract data type.**

For Example: For driving a car, you only use the essential features without knowing in details the internal mechanism of the system. You can apply brake to stop the car, press accelerator to speed up the car and press clutch to change the gears.

Do you ever think what changes are taking place in the machinery part of the engine? The answer is simply No. This act of driving a car is termed as **abstraction**.

1.4 ENCAPSULATION

Encapsulation is the system of wrapping up of data and functions into a single unit (called class).

For Data Hiding **Encapsulation** run on an important **OOP** concept. In Object Oriented Programming (OOP), data cannot move freely from method to method. They are kept in the corresponding classes in such a way that they will not be accessible to the outside world except by using them through the related methods.

It is the most important feature of a class. The functions used in a class can only access the data items. These functions provide interface between data items of the objects and the calling program.

Such insulation of data, which cannot be accessed directly outside class premises although they are available in the same program, is known as **DATA HIDING.**

1.5 POLYMORPHISM

The literal meaning of Polymorphism is "available in many forms". Suppose you have developed a method to perform the addition then it will find the sum of two numbers passed to the method. In case the passed arguments are strings, the function will produce the concatenated (joined) string.

Hence, Polymorphism is the ability of different objects to respond, each in its own way, to identical messages. It allows the use of different internal structure of the object by keeping the same external interface.

1.6 INHERITANCE

Inheritance can be defined as the process by which objects of one class can link and share some common properties of objects from another class.

An object of a class acquires some properties from the objects of another class. Superclass or base class is a class that used as basis for inheritance. Subclass or derived class is known as a class that inherits from a **superclass**.

BENEFITS OF OBJECT ORIENTED PROGRAMMING (OOP)

Some benefits of OOP are as listed below:

- You can create different modules in your project through objects.
- You can extend the use of existing class through inheritance.
- Using the concept data hiding can generate secured program.
- It is highly beneficial to solve complex problems.
- It is easy to modify and maintain software complexity.

INTRODUCTION TO JAVA

2.1 HISTORY OF JAVA

Java programming language was originally developed by **James Gosling** at **Sun Microsystems** (Broomfield, Colorado, USA) and released in 1995 as a core component of Sun Microsystems' **Java** platform. This language was initially called Oak (named after the Oak trees outside Gosling's office).The platform independence is one of the most significant advantage that **JAVA** has over other languages.

JAVA encapsulates many features of C++. Originally **JAVA** was designed to execute applets, downloaded while Web browsing. But gradually, the language has been gaining wide acceptance as a programming language, very often replacing C or C++.

2.2 BASIC FEATURES OF JAVA

JAVA possesses the following features:

- Java is not a purely Object Oriented Programming language.
- Java programs are both compiled and interpreted.
- It can access data from a local system as well as from net.
- Java programming is written within a class. The variables and functions are declared and defined with the class.
- Java programs can create Applets (the programs which run on Web-browsers).
- Java is case sensitive language. It distinguishes the upper case and lower case letters.

2.3 COMPILER AND INTERPRETER

All high level languages need to be converted into machine code so that the computer understands the program after taking the required inputs.

The conversion of high-level language to machine-level language can be done in two possible ways. It can be done either by using a Compiler or an Interpreter.

The software, by which the conversion of the high level instructions is performed line by line to machine level language, is known as an Interpreter. If an error is found on any line, further execution stops till it is corrected. This process of error correction is much easier but the program takes longer time to execute successfully.

SOURCE CODE -> COMPILER/INTERPRETER -> MACHINE CODE

However, if all the instructions are converted to machine level language at once and all the errors are listed together, then the software is known as Compiler. This process is much faster but sometimes it becomes difficult to debug all the errors together in a program.

The Java source code and Java bytecodes are compiles in **javac** command.

Compilation Syntax: **javac** filename.java

2.4 THE JVM

JAVA is a high level language (HLL)and the program written in HLL is compiled and then converted to an intermediate language called Byte Code. Byte code makes a Java program highly portable as its Bytes code can easily be transferred from one system to another. When this Byte code is to be run on any other system, an interpreter, known as Java Virtual Machine is needed which translates the byte code to machine code.

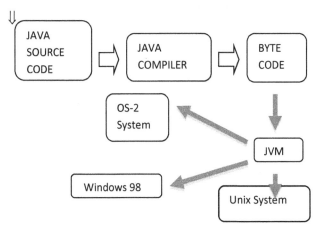

Java machine code varies from different platforms like

Windows 98, Unix System, etc. Hence, JVM acts as a virtual processor and converts the byte code to the machine code for concerning platform. That is why it is called **Java Virtual Machine**.

Three notions of **JVM** are: Implementation, instance and specification. The specification document describes what's required of JVM implementation. Single specification ensures all implementation are **interoperable**. Implementation program meets the requirements of the JVM specification. JVM Instance is implementation running in process that executes a program compiled into **Java bytecode**.

Thus, the Java machine uses compiler and interpreter too.

2.5 JAVA RUNTIME ENVIROMENT (JRE)

Java Runtime Environment is used to provide runtime environment. It is the implementation of **JVM**. It contains other files and set of libraries that used at runtime by **JVM**. It is a software package that contains what is required to run a Java program. It includes together Java Class Library Implementation and Java Virtual Machine implementation. The **Oracle Corporation**, which owns the Java trademark, distributes a Java Runtime environment with their Java Virtual Machine called **HotSpot**.

2.6 JAVA DEVELOPMENT KIT (JDK)

Java Development Kit (JDK) contains **JRE** and development tools. JDK Tools such as the compilers and debuggers are necessary for developing applications and applets.

Java Libraries in JDK 1.3

Java Development Kit (JDK) contains a Java Class Library for different purposes. Some useful packages in it are mentioned below:

- **java.io** : to support classes to deal with input & output statements.

- **java.lang** : to support classes containing String, Character, Math, Integer,Thread etc.

- **java.net** : to support classes for network related operations and dealing with URL (Uniform Resource Locator)

- **java.txt** : for supporting text elements such as date, times and currency etc.

- **java.math** : to support mathematical functional such as square roots (integer & decimal both)

- **java.applet** : to support classes to generate applet – specific environment

- **java.awt** : to support abstract window tool kit and managing GUI (Graphic User Interface)

2.7 RESERVED WORDS

Reserved words or keywords are those words which are preserved with the system. These words cannot be applied as a variable name in any program. Java also has reserved words. Some of the reserved/key words are listed below:

case	switch	int	void	default
do	break	double	import	boolean
try	const	long	class	char
catch	if	new	package	goto
for	else	byte	static	throws
while	short	public	private	float

Comment Statements in Java Programming

There are some cases where it becomes difficult for a user to understand the logic applied in a program particularly when any other person has developed it. In such cases, the programmer keeps mentioning the purpose and action being taken in different steps by applying comment statement in the program.

There are three ways to give a comment in Java programming.

> 1. // : used for single line comment
>
> 2. /* comments to be written */ : used for multi line comment

3. /** documenting comment */

Output Statement in Java Programming

System.out.println() and **System.out.print()** are the statements that are used to get the output of the program or to display messages on the screen.

While using **System.out.println()** statement, the cursor skips the line and passes to the next line after displaying the required result.

And, when you use **System.out.print()** statement, the cursor remains on the same line after displaying the result.

Syntax: System.out.println("Welcome to Java");
    System.out.println("The product of two numbers is" +a);

Note:

- The message is to be written within double quotes (" ") enclosed   within braces.
- When a message is to be displayed along with a variable, then they are to be separated with '+' (plus) sign.

DATA TYPES AND TOKENS IN JAVA

3.1 DATA TYPES

Data types are predefined **types** of **data,** which are supported by the programming language. It specifies the size and type of values that can be stored in a variable. In Java Programming we have to deal with various types of data, hence it becomes necessary for a programmer to select an appropriate data type according to the data taken in a program.

The data type has been divided into two types:

• Primitive Type
• Non-Primitive Type

Primitive Data Types

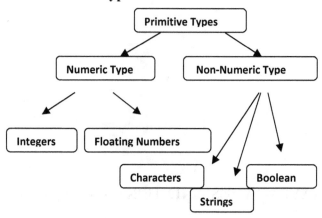

Primitive data types are pre-defined or built-in data types, which are independent of any other type. For eg. int, long, float, double etc.

Integer Type

Integer types can hold whole numbers such as 123 and −96. The values size can depend on stored integer type that we choose. It does not contain decimal point. There are two types of declarations under this heading:

- int : applied for short integer number.

    Bit size -> 32 bits, Format -> int a; a=10; or int a=10;

- long : applied for large integer number.

    Bit size -> 64 bits, Format -> long b; b=345678; or

long b=345678;

Floating Type

Floating point data types are used to represent numbers with a fractional part. There are two types of declarations under this heading:

• float : applied for small range of decimal values.

Bit size -> 32 bits, Format -> float m; m=32.65; or float m=32.65;

• double : applied for wide range of decimal values.

Bit size -> 64 bits, Format -> double n; n=0.0006547839; or   double n=0.0006547839;

Character Type

It stores character constants in the memory and contains a single character. A character is enclosed in single quotes (' ').Strings are enclosed in double quotes(" ").

The character types in Java are as follows:

Non Numeric	Character type	Bit Size	Format
Single character	Char	16 bits(2 bytes)	char c; c='A'; char d; d='*'; char c ='A';
More than one character/a word/a sentence	String	More than 16 bits	String a; a="College";

Boolean Type

Boolean data types are used to store values with two states: true or false. These are non-figurative constants. You can use Boolean type variable to set true or false in order to ensure whether a logical condition is satisfied or not. It assumes one of the values true or false without quotes.

For Example: boolean flag=true; or boolean flag=false;

Non-Primitive Data Type

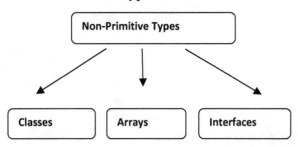

Classes

A class, in the context of Java, are templates that are used to create objects, and to define **object** data types and methods.

For Example:

public class MyFirstJavaProgram {

/*

   This is my first java program.

   This will print 'Welcome' as the output.

*/

public static void main (String[] args){

System.out.println("Welcome"); // prints Welcome

}

   }

Let's look at how to save the file, compile, and run the program−

- Open notepad and add the code as above.

- Save the file as: MyFirstJavaProgram.java.

- Open a command prompt window and go to the directory where you saved the class. Assume it's C:\.

- Type 'javac MyFirstJavaProgram.java' and press enter to compile your code. If no errors in code then command prompt will process to next line. Then, type ' java   MyFirstJavaProgram ' and press enter to run your program.

- You will be able to see ' Welcome ' printed on the window.

We will study later about Arrays in chapter 7

3.2 JAVA TOKENS

Each individual character used in a java statement is known as Java Token.

Types of Java Tokens

- Literals

- Identifiers

- Assignments

- Punctuators

- Operators

Literals (Constants)

These are the constants used in a Java program. Java uses the literals classified in the following ways:

Integer Literals : These are the whole numbers having positive or negative values. e.g. 15, 256,etc.

Real Literals : They represent numbers with decimal points. e.g. 24.6, 0.0045, etc.

Character Literals : The constants which are alphanumeric in nature are called character literals. e.g. 'A', 'b', '1', '*' etc.

String Literals : String is a set of alphanumeric characters.

 e.g. "Year 2017", etc.

Identifiers (Variables)

Identifiers are also called variables in Java programming. A variable is a named memory location, which contains a value. A variable can be treated by any combination of letters without spaces. We can declare more than one variables of the same type in a statement.

Syntax: datatype variable name;

e.g. int a; float a,b,c;

Assignments

Assignment token assigns the value on its right to the operand on its left. To **assign** object references **operator** can also be used.

e.g. int speed = 0; int gear = 1;

Punctuators

Punctuators are the punctuation signs used in Java. Some punctuators are : ; , ? etc.

Separators

These are special characters that are used in Java to separate the characters or variables.

e.g. (,),{,},[,] etc.

Operators

The operators are the symbols used to perform arithmetical or logical operations in Java programming. e.g. +,-,*,/,||,&&,<,> etc.

Note: We have Detail Explain about **Operators** in Next Chapter

OPERATORS AND EXPRESSIONS

I An operator is basically a symbol or token, which performs logical or arithmetical operations and gives meaningful result. The values which are involved in the operation, are termed as operands.

For example :[a + b * c] where a b and c are operands, + and * are the operators.

4.1 TYPES OF OPERATORS

Basically, there are three types of operators in Java which are as follows:

- **Arithmetical**

- **Relational**

- **Logical**

ARITHMETICAL OPERATORS

The operators, which are applied to perform arithmetical calculations in a program, are known as arithmetical operators like +,-,*,etc.

Arithmetical Expression:

An arithmetical expression may contain variables, constants and arithmetical operators together to produce a meaningful result.

e.g. a+b,x-10,b*b-4*a*c etc.

Arithmetical Statement:

If an arithmetical expression is assigned to a variable then it is known as an arithmetical statement.

Syntax: Variable = Arithmetical Expression;

e.g. x = a + b, z=b*b-4*a*c

Types of Arithmetical Operators

- Unary Operator

- Binary Operator

- Ternary Operator

Unary Operator

Unary operator can also be known as arithmetical operator which can be applied with a single operand. e.g. +,-,++ etc.

Unary Increment and Decrement Operators:

Unary Increment Operator (++) increases the value of an operand by one whereas Unary Decrement Operator (--) decreases the value of an operand by one.

Example:

1. $i = i + 1$

By applying increment operator it can be written as i++ or ++i

2. $j = j - 1$

By applying decrement operator it can be written as j-- or --j

Unary Increment/Decrement Operators:

- Prefix

- Postfix

Prefix

When increment or decrement operators are applied before the operand, it is known as prefix operators. This operator works on the principle **'CHANGE BEFORE ACTION'**. It means the value of the variable changes before the action takes place.

Example : p = 5;

p = ++p * 4; gives the result 24 as p increases by 1 before the operation performed.

p = --p * 4; gives the result 16 as p decreases by 1 before the operation is being performed.

Postfix

When increment or decrement operators are applied after the operand, it is known as postfix operators. This operator works on the principle **'CHANGE AFTER THE ACTION'**. It means the value of the variable changes after performing the operation.

Example : p = 5;

p = p++ * 4; gives the result 20 as p increases by 1 after the operation performed.

p = p-- * 4; gives the result 20 as p decreases by 1 after the operation is being performed.

Binary Arithmetic Operators

An arithmetic operator, which deals with two operands is known as Binary Arithmetic Operators. e.g a + b, a – b, etc.

Ternary Operators (Conditional Operator)

Ternary Operators takes three operands. It is also called conditional operator because the value assigned to a variable depends upon a logical expression.

Syntax: variable = (test expression)? Expression 1:Expression 2;

The variable contains the result of expression 1 if the test condition is true otherwise expression 2.

e.g. a = 4; b = 2;

max = (a>b)? a:b;

Here, the condition is true so the output will be 4 as the value of a is 4.

Nested Ternary Operator

You can use ternary operator in nested form as shown below :

e.g. Program to find maximum among three numbers:

   int a = 4, b = 10, c = 2;

max = (a>b)?   (a>c)? a:b   : (b>c)? b:c;

Test condition   Expression 1   Expression 2

Since, the test condition is false, it will operate expression 2 which enables value 12 to be stored in max. Hence, max = 12.

RELATIONAL OPERATORS

Relational operators compare the values of the variables and return a boolean value in terms of 'True' or 'False' (i.e. 0 or 1). **Java** has six **relational operators that are** < , > , <= , >= , == , and != .

LOGICAL OPERATORS

Java uses logical operators AND(&&), OR(||) or NOT(!). These operators yield 1 or 0 depending upon the output of different expressions.

e.g. (a>b)&&(a>c),!(a==b)

Note: If a statement contains all the three logical operators then NOT operator will perform first.

BITWISE OPERATORS

Bitwise operators use byte, short, int and long type operands. However, float and double types are not allowed.

e.g. & - Bitwise AND

   | - Bitwise OR

   ^ - Bitwise XOR

   << - Left Shift

   >> - Left Shift

4.2 EXPRESSIONS

When you write a program in Java, it is necessary to represent the arithmetical expressions into Java expressions.

Mixed Expression

An expression which includes different types of variables or values to yield a result is called as Mixed Expression.

e.g. int a; float b; double c;

double z = a + b * c;

Implicit Type Conversion

In mixed expression, the data type of the result gets converted automatically into its higher type without intervention of the user. This type conversion is known as Implicit Type Conversion.

Explicit Type Conversion

When the data type gets converted to another type after user intervention, the type conversion is known as Explicit Type Conversion.

e.g. int a, b;

float x = (float) (a+b);

CONDITIONAL AND DECISION MAKING STATEMENTS

In the first part of the chapter, we will discuss about unconditional statements, which will help to give a detailed idea of writing Java instructions in a program.

In order to perform a specified task in a program you need to provide some values, which can be used during execution of the program. The statement, which accepts the values from the users, is known as input statement. Java provides various ways to use input statements in programming. They are as follows:

- By assigning the values

- By using input streams

- By using Command line arguments

5.1 PROGRAMMING BY USING ASSIGNMENT STATEMENT

By using assignment statement, you can take values of data of your own or mentioned in the program.

Example: A program in Java to find the sum of two numbers using

assignment statement.

public class sum

{

public static void main (String args[])

{

int a,b,c; c=0;

a=15;b=45;

c=a+b;

System.out.println("The sum of the two numbers ="+c);

```
    }

    }
```

Output:

The sum of the two numbers = 60.

5.2 PROGRAMMING USING STREAMS

Package in Java is basically a collection of classes. Each package includes related built-in functions, which may be used while developing programming logic.

Buffer

CPU or processor is the fastest device in a computer. Other peripheral devices are comparatively slower then processor. Due to speed differences it becomes difficult to have data communication between processor and peripheral devices. Hence, a high speed memory is applied between I/O devices and processor used as a bridge to synchronize their speeds. This high-speed temporary storage (cache memory) is termed as Buffer. You need to activate the buffer before any input/output operation.

Activating Buffer in Java

InputStreamReader <object name1> = new InputStreamReader (System.in);

BufferedReader <object name2> = new BufferedReader (<object name1>)

OR

DataInputStream<object name> = new DataInputStream(System.in);

Main function

The next step is to declare a main function as given below:

public static void main (string args[])throws IOException

The main function is issued to execute a program. Thereafter, throws IOException eliminates I/O errors in the program(if any). It passes a report on I/O errors to the exception handler of Java System.

5.3 DECLARATIONS WHILE USING STREAMS

1. At first Java library package needs to be defined.

   Syntax: import java.io.*; or

   import java.io.lang or may be both the packages

2. Two statements are essentially needed, when you are using Input stream to activate buffer.

   DataInputStream in = new DataInputStream(System.in);

   OR

   public static void main(String args[])throws IOException

   InputStreamReader read = new InputStreamReader(System.in);

BufferedReader in = new BufferedReader(read);

3. A message is to be displayed before Input statement in order to enable input editor.

Syntax: System.out.println("Enter your name");

4. The Syntax of Input statement in Java programming:

n = Integer.parseInt(in.readLine());

This statement will accept only integer from the user whereas :

n = Float.parseFloat(in.readLine());

will accept fractional numbers from the user.

Example: A Java program to accept perpendicular and base of a Right angled triangle

calculating and displaying the hypotenuse and area of the triangle.

import java.io.*;

```java
public class Triangle

{

public static void main(String args[])throws
IOException

{

float p,b;

double area=0,hyp=0;

InputStreamReader read = new
InputStreamReader(System.in);

BufferedReader in = new BufferedReader(read);

System.out.println("Enter perpendicular and
base");

p=Float.parseFloat(in.readLine());

b=Float.parseFloat(in.readLine());

hyp=Math.sqrt(p*p+b*b);

area=(float)1/2*p*b;

System.out.println("Hypotenuse ="+hyp);
```

```
System.out.println("Area ="+area);

}

}
```

5.4 DECISION MAKING IN JAVA

Sometimes our program needs to take a decision based on whether a particular condition has occurred or not. Then our program will execute certain statements based on this decision.

Decision making in Java can be achieved using any of the following statements:

- if statement
- switch statement
- conditional operator statement

if statement

You can use if statement to check a specified condition. It performs a course of action if the condition is true otherwise, the action is ignored.

Syntax: if(condition)

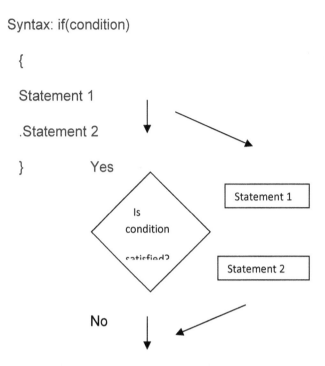

{

Statement 1

.Statement 2

}

If the statement is true the statements (statement 1 and statement 2) are executed. If the condition is false the control ignores the statements and passes to the next line of the program.

Example:

```
public class IfStatement
{
public static void main(String args[])
  {
    //Declaring a variable "test" and initializing it with a value 10
```

```
    int test=10;

    //Checking if "test" is greater than 5
      if(test>5)

      {
          //This block will be executed only if "test" is greater
than 5
          System.out.println("Success");
      }

      //The if block ends.
      System.out.println("Executed successfully");
   }
}
```

Output: Executed successfully

if-**else statement**

Here if the condition is true, the code which is written inside the curly brackets {} of the if block will be executed. If the condition is false, the code which is written inside the curly brackets {} of the else block will be executed.

Syntax:

```
 if(condition)

 {
    Statements which will be executed if the condition
is                                              true
 }
```

else

{

Statements which will be executed if the condition

is   false

}

Statements that need to be executed always

Example: public class IfElseStatement

```
{
public static void main(String args[])
{
//Declaring a variable "test" and initializing it with a value
10
int test=10;

//Checking if "test" is greater than 5
if(test>5)
{
//This block will be executed only if "test" is greater than 5
   System.out.println("Success");
}
else
{
 //This block will be executed only if "test" is not greater
than 5
   System.out.println("Failure");

}

//The if else blocks ends.
System.out.println("Executed successfully");
 }
}
```

Output: Success

Executed successfully

if else-if ladder

Conditions are calculated from top. 1st if(condition-x) will evaluate and if it's true, the code inside the if block will execute else if(condition-x) is false then else if (condition-y) will evaluate and If(condition-y) is true, then code inside that else-if block will execute or else If(condition-y) is false then else if(condition-z) will evaluate. This will go on like this.

If none of the conditions are true, the code inside the else block will execute.

Example:

```
if(condition-x)

{

  Statements    execute    if    condition-x    is    true

}


else if (condition-y)

{

  Statements execute if condition-y is true

}

.
```

.

.

else if(condition-z)

{

  Statements execute if condition-z is true

}

else

{

  Statements execute if none of the conditions in

condition-x, conditiony,...condition-z are true.

}

Statements execute always

Example:

```
public class IfElseIfLadder
{
public static void main(String args[])
{
    //Declaring a variable "test" and initializing it with a value
2
    int test=2;

    if(test==1)
    {
       //This block will be executed only if "test" is equal to 1
       System.out.println("Hello");
    }
    else if(test==2)
    {
       //This block will be executed only if "test" is equal to 2
       System.out.println("Hi");

    }
    else if(test==3)
```

```
    {
        //This block will be executed only if "test" is equal to 3
        System.out.println("Good");
    }
    else
    {
        System.out.println("No Match Found");
    }
  }
}
```

Output: Hi

Nested if…else statement

When you combine multiple if / if-else /if-else-if ladders then lot sequence decisions are involved. You have to take care of program executes, instructions when sequence conditions are encountered.

Example:

```
public class NestedIf

{

    public static void main(String args[])

    {

        //Declaring a variable a and initializing it with a value 5

        int a=3;

        //Declaring a variable b and initializing it with a value 3

        int b=3;
```

```java
if(a==5)

{

    //This block will be executed only if "a" is equal to 5

    if(b==3)

    {

        /*This block will be executed only if

        a is equal to 5   and b is equal to 3 */

        System.out.println("Hi, a is 5 and b is 3");



    }

    else

    {

        /*This block will be executed only if

        a is equal to 5 and b is some value other than 3 */

System.out.println("Hi, a is 5 and b is some value other than 3");

    }

}

else if(a==4)
```

```
{

    //This block will be executed only if a is 4

    System.out.println("Hi, a is 4");


}

else if(a==3)

{

    //This block will be executed only if "a" is 3


    if(b==3)

    {

/*This block will be executed only if a is equal to 3 and b is
equal   to 3 */

   System.out.println("Hi, a is 3 and b is 3");

    }

    else if(b==2)

    {

        /*This block will be executed only if

        a is equal to 3 and b is equal to 2 */

        System.out.println("Hi, a is 3 and b is 2");
```

```
        }


    }

    else

    {

        /*This block will be executed only if

        a is some value other than 5,4,3*/


System.out.println("Hi, a is some value other than 5,4,3");

    }

  }

}
```

Output: Hi, a is 3 and b is 3

Switch case statement

Switch case statement is a multiple branching statement. In this system the control jumps to perform a particular action out of a number of actions depending upon a switch value. A switch statement is associated with a number of blocks. Each block is defined under a specific case. The control gets transferred to a particular case, which matches with the given switch value. Each case ends with a break statement, which can be used as a case terminator. Break statement passes the control out of the switch block.

You can use a special case called default case which is automatically followed if no case matches with the given switch value.

Example: A Java program to accept two numbers and find the sum, difference or product according to user's choice.

```
import java.io.*;

public class choice

{

public static void main(String args[])throws
IOException

{

int a,b,ch;
```

```java
InputStreamReader read = new
InputStreamReader(System.in);

BufferedReader in = new BufferedReader(read);

System.out.println("Enter two numbers");

a=Integer.parseInt(in.readLine());

b=Integer.parseInt(in.readLine());

System.out.println("Enter 1 to add,2 to sub.,3 to
mult");

System.out.println("Enter your choice");

ch=Integer.parseInt(in.readLine());

switch(ch)

{

case 1:

System.out.println("The sum of two nos.="+(a+b));

break;

case 2:

System.out.println("The diff. of two nos.="+(a-b));

break;

case 3:
```

```java
System.out.println("The product of two
nos.="+(a*b);

break;

default:

System.out.println("It is a wrong choice");

}

}

}
```

LOOPING

6.1 LOOPING STRUCTURE

A looping structure contains the following parts:

- Control Variable
- Body of the loop
- Test Condition
- Step Value

6.2 TYPES OF LOOPS

Types of Loops in Java:

- for loop
- while loop
- do while loop

for loop

We can perform any conditional repetitive type of flow very easily with the help of for loop. It is used for a fixed number of iterations.

Syntax: for(initial value; final value; step value)

```
{

task to be performed

}
```

Example: A Java program to print all natural numbers from 1 to 5.

```
public class num

{

public static void main(String args[])

{

int a;

for(a=1;a<=5;a++)

{

System.out.println(a);

}
```

}

Output: 1

    2

    3

    4

    5

Nested for loop

When you apply a for loop within another for loop, the structure is termed as nested for loop.

Example: A Java program to display the given pattern using for loop.

1

1 2

1 2 3

```
public class pattern

{

public static void main(String args[])

{

int a;
```

```
for(a=1;a<=3;a++)

{

for(b=1;b<=a;b++)

{

System.out.print(b);

System.out.println();

}

}

}
```

while loop

while loop repeats a statement or group of statements while a given condition is true. It tests the condition before executing the loop body. The loop will continue executing till the test condition is true.

Syntax: while(condition)

```
    {

    Statements to execute

    }
```

Example: A program in Java to display a message on the screen 10 times by   using while statement.

```
public class msg

{

public static void main(String args[])

{

int i=1;

while(i<=10)

{

System.out.println("Welcome to Java Programming.");

i++;

}

}
```

Infinite while loop

In a while loop, if a user does not provide increment/decrement expression it becomes infinite loop. The loop repeats infinitely as the test condition always remains true.

```
int i=1;
```

```
while(i<=10)

{

s=s+i;

}
```

Nested while loop

Nested while loop can be known as while loop used within another while loop.

Example: A Java program to display the given pattern using while loop.

```
1

1 2

1 2 3
```

```
public class pattern

{

public static void main(String args[])

{

a=1;
```

```
while(a<=3)

{

b=1;

while(b<=a)

{

System.out.print(b);

b++;

}

System.out.println();

a++;

}
```

Do-while loop

Do-while loop is used in a program where number of iterations is not fixed. In this system, the control enters the loop without checking any condition, executes the given steps and then checks the condition for further continuation of the loop.

Thus, this type of loop executes the tasks at least once. If the condition is not satisfied, then the control exits from the loop.

Syntax: do

   {

   task to do

   }

   while(condition);

Example: A Java program to find the factorial of 10.

```java
public class factorial

{

public static void main(String args[])

{

int i,f;i=1;f=1;

do

{

f=f*i;

i++;

}

while(i<=10);
```

Sytem.out.println("The factorial of 10 =" +f);

}

}

Use of break statement

Sometimes, it is needed to stop a loop suddenly when a condition is satisfied. A break statement is used for unusual termination of a loop.

Syntax: while(condition)

   {

   execution continues

   if(another condition is true)

   break;

   ------;

   ------;

  }

Use of continue statement

The statement continue, is just the opposite of break statement. As soon as the continue statement is executed in a loop, the control skips rest of the statement for that value and resumes for the next iteration.

Syntax: while(condition)

```
{
 Statement 1
 ------;
 ------;
 if(another condition)
 continue;
 Statement 2
 -------;
 -------;
}
```

ARRAY

In Java programming, you may need to structure the memory to store numerous data items by applying minimum set of variables and by using optimum memory space. It becomes necessary to store data within the memory in the most convenient and economical way.

Java array is an object that contains elements of similar data type. It is a data structure where we store similar elements. We can store only fixed set of elements in a java array.

Index based Array is in java,

Array First element is stored at 0 index.

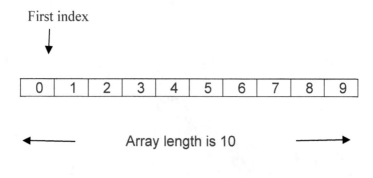

7.1 TYPES OF ARRAY

• **Single Dimensional Array**

• **Double Dimensional Array**

Single Dimensional Array

Single Dimensional Array is also known when the elements are specified by a single subscript,

Syntax to Declare Single Dimensional Array

• dataType[] arr; (or)

• dataType []arr; (or)

• dataType arr[];

7.2 DECLARATION OF AN ARRAY IN JAVA

Array in java can be Declare like:

arrayVar= new datatype[size];

Example of Single Dimensional Java Array

1. class TestSingleArray{

2. public static void main(String args[]){

3.

4. int a[]=new int[5]; //declaration and instantiation of int

5. a[0]=10; //initialization a[?] with numbers

6. a[1]=20;

7. a[2]=70;

8. a[3]=40;

9. a[4]=50;

10.

11. //printing array

12. for(int i=0;i<a.length;i++)//length is the property of array

13. System.out.println(a[i]);

14.

15. }}

Output: 10

    20

    70

    40

    50

Instantiate and initializing the java array together can be declared as:

1. class Test1Instantiateandinitializating{

2. public static void main(String args[]){

3.

4.   int a[]={33,3,4,5}; //declaration, instantiation and initialization int

5.

6.   //printing array

7.   for(int i=0;i<a.length;i++) //length is the property of array

8.   System.out.println(a[i]);

9.

10. }}

Output:

    33

    3

    4

    5

7.3 PASSING AN ARRAY TO METHOD

We can pass the java array to method so that we can reuse the same logic on any array.

1. class Test2PassingMethod{

2. static void min(int arr[]){

3. int min=arr[0];

4. for(int i=1;i<arr.length;i++)

5.   if(min>arr[i])

6.   min=arr[i];

7.

8. System.out.println(min);

9. }

10.

11. public static void main(String args[]){

12.

13. int a[]={33,2,4,5};

14. min(a);//passing array to method

15. }}

Output:2

Double Dimensional Array

In such case, data is stored in row and column based index (also known as matrix form).

Syntax :   dataType[][] arrayRefVar; (or)
dataType [][]arrayRefVar; (or)
dataType arrayRefVar[][]; (or)
dataType []arrayRefVar[];

Example to instantiate 2-dimensional array:

int[][] arr = new int[3][3];//3 row and 3 column

Example to initialize 2-dimensional array:

arr[0][0]=1;
arr[0][1]=2;
arr[0][2]=3;
arr[1][0]=4;
arr[1][1]=5;
arr[1][2]=6;
arr[2][0]=7;
arr[2][1]=8;

arr[2][2]=9;

Example of 2-dimensional array:

```
1.        class Testarray3Dimensional{
2.        public static void main(String args[]){
3.
4.        //declaring and initializing 2D array
5.        int arr[][]={{1,2,3},{2,4,5},{4,4,5}};
6.
7.        //printing 2D array
8.        for(int i=0;i<3;i++){
9.         for(int j=0;j<3;j++){
10.          System.out.print(arr[i][j]+" ");
11.         }
12.         System.out.println();
13.        }
14.
15.       }}
```

Output: 1 2 3
      2 4 5
      4 4 5

7.4 BASIC OPERATIONS ON JAVA

Arrays provide the following basic operations:

• Searching

- Sorting
- Insertion
- Deletion
- Merging

Search

It is a process to determine whether a given item is present in the array or not. This can be done by two ways:

- Linear Search
- Binary Search

Linear Search

It is one of the simplest technique in which the searching of an item begins at the start of an array(i.e. 0th position of the array). The process continues one another, where each element of the array is checked and compared with a given data item till the end of the array location is reached. This process is also called as **Sequential Search**.

Binary Search

It is the another technique to search an element in the given array by using minimum possible time. Searching takes place in either half of the array by further dividing it into two halves.

However, the binary search can be applied only when the array elements are sorted into a sequence(ascending/descending).It always compares the element to be searched with the middle element of the sorted array. If the middle member is smaller then, the search is carried out in upper half, otherwise the search continues in the lower half. The middle element of the either half is compared with the search item. This process is repeated till the search terminates.

18	32	50	56	65	79	88
0th	1st	2nd	3rd	4th	5th	6th

First   **Mid**   **Last**

Step 1: First=0,Last=6,Mid=(First+Last)/2=(0+6)/2=3

Step 2: num[Mid]=num[3]=55

    55>31

Since, 55 is greater therefore search will take place in the first half of the array.

Step 3: Last=Mid-1 = 3-1=2

(In case, the number to be searched is greater than the mid value then, First=Mid+1).

Mid=(First+Last)/2 = (0+2)/2=1

Num[Mid]= num[1]=31

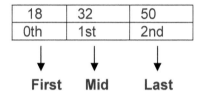

Sorting

It is a process of arranging data in a specified order which may be either ascending or descending.

- Selection Sort
- Bubble Sort

Selection Sort

This is one of the techniques to sort the given data item in a specified order(ascending/descending).

Suppose you have to arrange numbers in ascending orders from unsorted data.

Step 1: At first, the smallest number is selected through iteration from the unsorted data list. This number is interchanged with the number at 0th position (i.e. 16 comes from 6th position to 0th position and 45 goes to 6th position from 0th position).

45	98	50	57	90	28	16	78
0th	1st	2nd	3rd	4th	5th	6th	7th

Step 2: Find the next smallest element from 1st position onward(i.e.28). Interchange it with 1st position element.

16	98	50	57	90	28	45	78
0th	1st	2nd	3rd	4th	5th	6th	7th

Step 3: Find the next smallest element from 2nd position onward(i.e.45).Interchange it with 2nd position element.

16	28	50	57	90	98	45	78
0th	1st	2nd	3rd	4th	5th	6th	7th

Step 4: Find the next smallest element from 3rd position onward(i.e.50).Interchange it with 3rd position element.

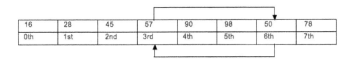

16	28	45	57	90	98	50	78
0th	1st	2nd	3rd	4th	5th	6th	7th

Step 5: Find the next smaller element from 4th position onward(i.e.57). Interchange it with 4th position element.

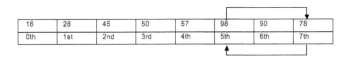

16	28	45	50	90	98	57	78
0th	1st	2nd	3rd	4th	5th	6th	7th

Step 6: Find the next smaller element from 5th position onward(i.e.78). Interchange it with 5th position element.

16	28	45	50	57	98	90	78
0th	1st	2nd	3rd	4th	5th	6th	7th

Step 7: Find the next smaller element from 6th position onward(i.e.90). Interchange it with 6th position element.

16	28	45	50	57	78	90	98
0th	1st	2nd	3rd	4th	5th	6th	7th

Thus, the numbers are arranged in ascending order using **Selection Sort**.

Bubble Sort

This technique is most widely used for sorting elements in a single dimensional array. In this technique, array is sequentially scanned several times and during each iteration the pairs of consecutive elements are compared and interchanged into a specific order(ascending/descending). It is an easy technique but consumes lot of time when the number of exchanges is much high.

Technique to sort the numbers using bubble sort

Arranging the elements in ascending order:

10	7	25	4	12
0th	1st	2nd	3rd	4th

Elements 10 and 7 are compared. Both are interchanged as 10>7.

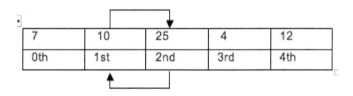

7	10	25	4	12
0th	1st	2nd	3rd	4th

Elements 10 and 25 are compared but not interchanged as 10<25.

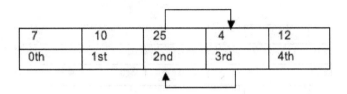

7	10	25	4	12
0th	1st	2nd	3rd	4th

Elements 25 and 4 are compared and interchanged as 25>4.

10	7	4	25	12
0th	1st	2nd	3rd	4th

Elements 25 and 12 are compared and interchanged as 25>12.

Thus, the numbers are arranged in ascending order using **Bubble Sort**.

Insertion

To perform an **insertion sort**, begin at the left-most element of the array and invoke Insert to insert each element encountered into its correct position. The ordered sequence into which the element is inserted is stored at the beginning of the array in the set of indices already examined.

CLASSES, OBJECTS AND METHODS

8.1 CLASSES IN JAVA

A class is a blueprint from which individual objects are created.

Example: public class boy

```
{
    String name;

    int age;

    void study(){

    }

    void hungry(){

    }
```

```
void sleeping(){

}

}
```

A class contain any following variables type.

- **Local variables** − Local variables can be defined inside methods, constructors or blocks.

- **Instance variables** − Variables declare within a class but outside any method and Variables initialized within class are instantiated is Instance variables. Variables can accessed from inside of any method, constructor or blocks of particular class.

- **Class variables** − With the static keyword, within a class or outside any method are Class variables.

8.2 CREATING AN OBJECT

An object is created from a class and new keyword is used to create new objects.

Creating an object from a class there are three steps−

- **Declaration** – A variable name with an object type.

- **Instantiation** – 'new' keyword used to create an object.

- **Initialization** – 'new' keyword followed by constructor. This call initializes new object.

Example: public class Boy{

```
public boy(String name){

System.out.println("Name is:" +name);

}

public static void main(String args[]){

Boy obj = new Boy("Ram");

}

}
```

Output:

Name is: Ram

8.3 METHODS

A program module used simultaneously at different instances in the program is known as Methods.

8.4 CREATING METHOD

Syntax: public static int user(int a,int b){

//body

}

Here,

- **public static** − modifier

- **int** − return type

- **user** − name of the method

- **a, b** − formal parameters

- **int a, int b** − list of parameters

Example: public static int max(int a,int b){

int max;

if(a>b){

```
max=a;

}

else{

max=b;

}

return max;

}
```

'this' keyword in Java

Sometimes, in a member method it is needed to use the object on which the method is called. Java system uses it with this keyword. The object on which the method is called can be reffered in the method with this.

Example: class keyword

```
{

int a,b;

void getvalue(int p,int q)
```

```
    {

    a=p;

    b=q;

    }

    void sum(keyword x, keyword y)

    {

    this.a=x.a+y.a;

    this.b=x.b+y.b;

    }

    void display()

    {

    System.out.println("sum of a"+a);

    System.out.println("sum of b"+b);

    }

    }
```

```
class calculate

{

public static void main(String args[])

{

keyword ob1 = new keyword();

keyword ob2 = new keyword();

keyword ob3 = new keyword();

ob1.getvalue(2,3);

ob2.getvalue(4,6);

ob3.sum(ob1,ob2);

ob3.display();

}

}
```

8.5 METHOD CALLING

There are two ways of a method calling.

- Method returns a value
- Returning nothing (no return value).

Method calling process is simple. When program invokes method, program control moved to called method. Then called method returns control to the caller in two conditions.

- First when return statement is execute, and
- Second when reached to method ending closing brace.

The void Keyword: It allows us to create methods which do not return a value.

8.6 METHOD OVERLOADING

It is known when a class has two or more methods with the same name but with different parameters.

Example: public class MethodOverloading{

   public static void main(String[] args){

   int w=10;

   int x=5;

```java
double y=6.3;

double z=8.4;

int value1= miniVal (w, x);

double value2= miniVal(y, z);

// same type of function name with different parameters

System.out.println("Minimum value =" +value1);

System.out.println("Minimum value =" +value2);

}

// for integer type

public static int miniVal(int x1, int x2){

int mini;

if(x1>x2){

mini=n2;

}

else{
```

```java
    mini=x1;

    }

    return mini;

    }

    // for value function

    public static double miniVal (double x1, double
x2){

    double mini;

    if(x1>x2){

    mini=x2;

    }

    else{

    mini=x1;

    }

    double mini;

    }
```

}

8.7 METHOD OVERRIDING

Method overriding in java can be Know If child class (subclass) has same method as declared in the parent class.

Example: **class** schoolclass{

```
void run(){System.out.println("school is running");}
        }
        class classroom2 extends schoolclass{
        void run(){System.out.println("class
room is running");}
        public static void main(String args[]){
        classroom2 obj = new classroom2();
        obj.run();
        }
```

Can we override static method?

No, static method cannot be overridden because static method is bound with class whereas instance method is bound with object. Static belongs to class area and instance belongs to heap area. We cannot override java main method because main is a static method.

INTERFACES AND PACKAGES

9.1 INTERFACES

Interfaces are syntactically similar to classes, but you cannot create instance of an **Interface** and their methods are declared without any body. Interface is used to achieve complete **abstraction** in Java.

Syntax : interface interface_name{}

While, implementing interface in class, the word 'implement' should be used and the methods can have different statements inside them. A class can implement more than one interface.Whatever the methods is in interface, it should be used in the class otherwise, while compilation, error will occur.

Example: interface UseInterface

```
{

int a=20;

void use();

}

class Value implements UseInterface

 {

public void use()

{

System.out.println("The value of a="+a);

}

public static void main(String args[])

{

Value v = new Value();

v.use();
```

}

}

Output: The value of a=20

9.2 PACKAGES IN JAVA

A package is a group of classes, which can be imported to a program so that the user may exercise the implicit facility available in it.

A package in java program can be included by using import command.

E.g. import java.util.data

The util function is imported to utilize its in-**built data class.**

import java.util.*;

It allows all the classes of java.util package to be included.

Some basic packages which can be imported for various fundamental operations are:

java.io

java.util

java.awt

java.net

Java packages for Mathematical Calculations

For the mathematical functions, we can include import.java.lang.Math;

Some of the functions are mentioned below:

Function	Description	Format
sqrt(a)	Returns the square root of a positive number	Math.sqrt(a);
min(a,b)	Returns the smaller number between a and b	Math.min(a,b);
max(a,b)	Returns the greater number between a and b	Math.max(a,b) ;
abs(a)	Returns the absolute value of any numeric	Math.abs(a);
round(a)	Returns the rounded value upto the nearest integer	Math.round(a) ;
exp(a)	Returns an exponent value	Math.exp(a);
ceil(a)	Returns the rounded value to the higher	Math.ceil(a);

	integer	

User defined packages

Till now, we have discussed built in java packages. A package may be defined by the users to be used in various programming logic. These are known as user defined packages.

e.g. Package area;

   Class Rectangle

   {

   }

   Class square

   {

   }

The package name is area. All the classes within it are the members of area package.

9.3 ADVANTAGES OF JAVA PACKAGE

1) It is used to classify the interfaces and classes, so they can be maintain easily.

2) It is responsible for access protection.

3) Naming collision is removed.

4) It provides reusability of code.

5) You can create your own **Package** or extend already available **Package.**

CONSTRUCTORS

A constructor is a member function with a name as same as that of the class name used to initialize the instant variables of the objects.

10.1 TYPES OF CONSTRUCTOR

- Default Constructor

- Parameterized Constructor

- Copy Constructor

Default Constructor

A constructor which initializes instant variables of an object with definite values is known as Default Constructor.

Example: class Book{

/*This is my default constructor having no return type and name

same as class name.*/

Book(){

System.out.println("Default constructor");

}

public void mymethod()

{

System.out.println("void method of the class");

}

public static void main(String args[]){

Book obj = new Book();

obj.mymethod();

}

}

Output: Default Constructor

void method of the class

Parameterized Constructor

A constructor which is used to initialize the object variables by passing parametric values at the time of its creation is known as **Parameterized constructor.**

Example: class pconst{

int a,b;

pconst(int x,int y){

a=x;

b=y;

}

void display(){

System.out.println("The value of a=" +a);

System.out.println("The value of b=" +b);

}

}

Copy Constructor

Copy Constructor copies the values of instant variables of an object to another instant variables object.

Example: class copycon{

//class using parameterized and copy constructors;

int a,b;

copycon(int x,int y){

a=x;

b=y;

}

}

class abc{

public static void main(String args[]){

```
copycon ob=new copycon(5,8);

copycon ob1=ob;

}

}
```

Thread and Multithread in Java

THREAD

Thread is a single process to activate multiple processes running in background. It makes process simple to execute and look into files sequence based as coded.

11.1 LIFE CYCLE OF A THREAD

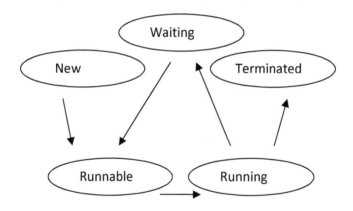

1.   **New :** A thread begins its life cycle in the new state. It remains in this state until the start() method is called on it.

2.   **Runnable :** After invocation of start() method on new thread, the thread becomes runable.

3.   **Running :** A method is in running thread if the thread scheduler has selected it.

4.   **Waiting :** A thread is waiting for another thread to perform a task. In this stage the thread is still alive.

5.   **Terminated :** A thread enter the terminated state when it complete its task.

11.2 MOSTLY USED METHODS OF THREAD CLASS

1. **run():** Perform action for a thread.
2. **start():** Starts execution of thread by calling run() method.
3. **stop()** : Stop's the thread.
4. **sleep():** For a specified time suspend thread.
5. **getPriority():** Priority of the thread returns.
6. **setPriority():** Priority of the thread changes.
7. **getName():** Name of the thread returns.
8. **setName():** Name of the thread changes.
9. **getId():** Id of the thread returns.
10. **suspend()** : Suspend the thread.
11. **resume()** : Resume the suspended thread.
12. **stop()** : Stop the thread.

11.3 CREATING A THREAD

There are two ways to create a thread:

1. Extending Thread class
2. Implementing Runnable interface.

Example by extending thread class

```
class MyThread extends Thread

{

public void run()

{

System.out.println("Concurrent    thread    started
running..");

}

}

class MyThreadDemo

{

public static void main(String args[])

{

MyThread th = new MyThread();
```

```
th.start();

}

}
```

Output: Concurrent thread started running..

Example by implementing Runnable interface

```
class Test implements Runnable{
public void run(){
System.out.println("Concurrent       thread       started
running..");
}

public static void main(String args[]){
Test x=new x();
Thread y =new Thread(y);
y1.start();
 }
}
```

Output: Concurrent thread started running..

11.4 MULTITHREADING

The Word Multithreading Mean, program contains two or more than two thread which runs parallel. Multithreading used because threads share a common memory area without allocating separate memory area to save more and also it takes less time than previous process.

Handling Exceptions and Errors

An exception is a problem that arises during the execution of a program. When an **Exception** occurs the normal flow of the program is disrupted and the program terminates abnormally, which is not recommended, therefore, these exceptions are to be handled.

Following are some scenarios where an exception occurs.

- When a user has entered an invalid data.

- When file cannot be found.

- When network connection is lost in middle of communications or the Java Virtual Machine runs out of memory.

These exceptions are caused by user, programmer and by physical resources that have failed in some method.

12.1 EXCEPTION HANDLING WITH TRY-CATCH

Try keyword contains a block of statements to perform. Any exception occurring within the try block is trapped. Hence, it is an error trapper. Further a report is to be passed to the exception handler about the error, which can be done by catch block.

The **finally** block contains the statements which are executed any way.

Syntax to use try-catch exception handler:

try

{

Set of statements

}

catch(exception(e)){

}

finally

{

Statement to execute any way

}

Example: import java.io.*;

```java
public class Test{

public static void main(String args[]){

try{

int a[]=new int[2];

System.out.println("Access    element    three    :"
+a[3]);

}catch(ArrayIndexOutOfBoundsException e){

System.out.println("Exception thrown :" +e);

}

System.out.println("Out of the block");

}

}
```

Output: java.lang.ArrayIndexOutOfBoundsException:
3

Out of the block

12.2 EXCEPTION HANDLING WITH THROWS KEYWORD

If you want that the system is to be reported for an error then you can apply throws keyword. A throws keyword is applied with function signature.

Example: public void getdata() throws IOException

This indicates, if an error occurs in the function related to I/O operation a report may be passed to the error handler.

Checked Exception

The classes that extend Throwable class except RuntimeException and Error are known as checked exceptions e.g.IOException, SQLException etc. Checked exceptions are checked at compile-time.

Unchecked Exception

The classes that extend RuntimeException are known as unchecked exceptions e.g.ArithmeticException,NullPointerException,ArrayInd exOutOfBoundsException etc. Unchecked exceptions are not checked at compile-time rather they are checked at runtime.

12.3   JAVA   EXCEPTION   HANDLING ADVANTAGES

- Exception handling is Helpful in the Separation of results for less complex and readable code. It is also more capable, in the logic that the testing of errors in the normal implementation path is not needed.

- Logical error types Exceptions can be group together with errors that are connected. It enables us to handle associated exceptions using single exception handler. An exception handler can catch exceptions of the class or any sub-class specified by its parameter.

- Exception handling allows related information to be caught at where an error occurs and to show it where it can be successfully controlled.

12.4 ERROR

Error is irrecoverable e.g. OutOfMemoryError, VirtualMachineError, etc.

Common Coding Errors:

- Syntax Error – Syntax errors are errors occurred in the syntax of a particular sequence of characters of a program.

- Logical Errors – Logical errors occur when there is a design flaw in your program.

- Runtime Errors – Runtime errors occur during the execution of the program.

12.5 DIFFERENCE BETWEEN ERROR AND EXCEPTIONS

ERRORS	EXCEPTIONS
Errors at run time cannot be known to compiler	Checked exception can be known and Uncheck cannot be known at run time
Error Occurs or caused when an application runs	Exceptions Occurs by the application itself
Errors in java are Mostly Uncheck type	Check and Uncheck are Two type of exceptions in Java

Questions and Answers

1. A program of Java that can be developed and executed by the users, is known as

   a> Application   b> Applet

   c> Object   d> none

2. Java Virtual Machine (JVM) is an

   a> Interpreter   b> Interpreter

   c> Machine code   d> Byte code

3. To find the square root of a number which of the following package is required?

   a> java.txt   b> java.math

   c> java.lang   d> java.net

4. Which of the following is not a Java reserved word?

a> private   b> public

c> break   d> character

5. The term used to correct the error in a program, is known as

a> bug   b> debugging

c> error removing   d> none

6. A constant which gives the exact representation of data is called

a> Variable   b> Literal

c> Identifier   d> Character

7. The statement n++ is equivalent to

a> ++n   b> n=n+1

c> n+1   d> none

8. What will be the output of a & b, if int a,b; a=10;b=++a?

a> 10,10   b> 10,11

c> 11,10   d> 11,11

9. What will be the output of a++; int a=-1?

a> 1   b> -1

c> 0   d> none

10. if condition is essentially formed by using

a> Arithmetic operators   b>
   Relational operators

c> Logical operators   d>   ternary
   operators

11. If(a!=b){

   c=a;

   }

   else

   {

   c=b;

   }

   can be written as

a> c=(b!=a)?a:b;   b> c=(a!=b)?a:b;

c> c=(a!=b)?b:a;   d> both a & b

12. Which element is represented with a[10]

a> 10th   b> 9th

c> 11th   d> none

13. The statement : int code[]={26,38,39,43};

a> Assign 38 to code[1]
b> b> Assign 26 to code[1]

c> Assign 39 to code[3]
d> d> none

14. A function with many definitions is known as

a> multiple function   b>function
   overloading

c> floating function   d> none

15. A function is invoked through a class type-

a> object   b> system

c> parameter   d> none

ANSWERS:

1. a   2. a   3. b   4. d   5. b

6. b   7. b   8. B   9. c   10. b

11. d   12. c   13. a   14. b   15. a